LET'S TALK ABOUT
FEELING GUILTY

by Joy Berry • Illustrated by Maggie Smith

Copyright© Joy Berry, 2022
Originally Published, 1995

All rights are reserved.

No part of this book can be duplicated or used without the prior written permission of the copyright owner, except for the use of brief quotations from the book.

For inquiries or permission requests contact the publisher.

Published by Joy Berry Enterprises
www.joyberryenterprises.com

Hello, my name is Sundance.

I live with Lily.

Sometimes Lily says or does something that hurts someone else's feelings.

Lily feels guilty.

Sometimes Lily breaks something that isn't hers.

Lily feels guilty.

Sometimes Lily does something she's not supposed to do.

Lily feels guilty.

Sometimes Lily doesn't play fair.

Lily feels guilty about cheating.

One time, Lily took something that didn't belong to her.

She also told a lie about it.

Lily felt guilty.

Guilt is the uncomfortable feeling you get when you've done something wrong.

When you feel guilty, you feel ashamed and embarrassed.

When you've done something wrong, you might want to pretend you didn't.

You might also want to hide what you've done wrong.

It's best not to cover up what is making you feel guilty.

When you've done something wrong, you might want to lie about it.

It's best not to.

It isn't fun to feel guilty.

But guilt can bring about something good if it helps you fix what you've done wrong.

You shouldn't ignore your guilty feelings.

Instead, admit that you've done something wrong.

When you feel guilty about hurting someone's feelings, try to make the person feel better.

When you feel guilty for breaking something, say you're sorry.

Try to replace or fix what has been broken.

When you feel guilty for disobeying, say you're sorry.

Then try not to disobey again.

When you feel guilty about lying, admit that you were dishonest.

Then tell the truth.

When you feel guilty about cheating, say you are sorry.

Then be sure to play fair the next time.

Nobody is perfect.

Everyone makes poor choices and feels guilty sometimes.

If you can admit to what you've done wrong and apologize, you'll feel less guilty.

Let's talk about... **Joy Berry!**

As the inventor of self-help books for kids, Joy Berry has written over 250 books that teach children about taking responsibility for themselves and their actions. With sales of over 80 million copies, Joy's books have helped millions of parents and their kids.

Through interesting stories that kids can relate to, Joy Berry's Let's Talk About books explain how to handle even the toughest situations and emotions. Written in a clear, simple style and illustrated with bright, humorous pictures, the Let's Talk About books are fun, informative, and they really work!

www.ingramcontent.com/pod-product-compliance
Lightning Source LLC
Chambersburg PA
CBHW081411070526
44583CB00020B/2771